LOVING YOURSELF FIRST

Cover Design by Merna Harrington
Editing by Merna Harrington
Photos courtesy of Pixabay.com
Copyright © 2015 by Merna Harrington
All rights reserved.

This book and story line may not be reproduced or transmitted in any form or by any means, electronic or mechanical, including photocopying, recording or by any information storage and retrieval system, without permission in writing from the publisher, except where permitted by law.

ISBN-13: 978-0692598948
ISBN10: 0692598944
First Edition First Printing

Dedication Page

This book is dedicated to anyone who feels as though they have lost themselves and aren't sure how to get back to the person they once knew, loved, and connected with on a daily basis. It is for those who never knew who they were, they just learned to adapt in a world of confusion. It is dedicated to those who may not recognize the person they have become because of internal and external expectations associated with society and everyday life. It is especially dedicated to those ones who love themselves enough to be held accountable for their own happiness, and once found, would love to see other's as happy as they are.

LOVING YOURSELF FIRST

~Contents~

Chapter 1 - Loving Yourself First...............1

Chapter 2 - Gather with Those Who Celebrate You...22

Chapter 3 – Becoming One with Yourself.........25

Chapter 4 – Heart Space...............38

Chapter 5 – You Are Love.......43

Enjoy the Journey.........................47

Infinite Self-Love....................................50

30 Day Journal...............52

Strengths & Weaknesses............82

WELCOME

First things first, I would like to say, you should be proud of yourself for investing in you! Thank you for taking the journey to "Loving Yourself First," You will be extremely happy you did! This book is about love; loving yourself first, and then all other things. We all will agree, it is always nice to show other's affection; letting them know that we care; that we are thinking about them, are proud of them, or just want to show compassion, sympathy, or empathy. However, wouldn't you also agree that we all need love and affection? Well, it is time we started loving ourselves first in order to fully understand, appreciate, and love all other things.

It is time to get back to ourselves, our true selves; the self that has been lost in the chaos of societal norms, pain, grief, oppression, poverty, low self-esteem, fear, and doubt. In getting back to ourselves, we have to remember who we were before we became the people our environments needed us to be; who we were before someone else mapped out our lives for us; before we decided to become carbon copies of one another in hopes of fitting in. IT'S TIME! TIME TO BEGIN LOVING OURSELVES FIRST! So come on in, take off your shoes, get comfortable, and be introduced to your AMAZING self. Enjoy the journey…

LOVING YOURSELF FIRST

Loving Myself

Before I started loving myself, I was in a lot of pain. I allowed people to treat me the way they wanted to treat me; I treated myself poorly, always beating myself up; I didn't understand my purpose in life and I was confused; I kept setting myself up for failure, and I would unintentionally sabotage any good thing that came to me.

I was hurting, which caused my children pain. I unintentionally hurt others by the decisions I made, not thinking about what I was doing to my inner self, as well as my outer environment. When you don't understand life; the meaning of life, and your purpose in the scheme of things, you are unable to see your true beauty and capabilities from within and all around you.

When I realized I was LOVE, and that love was the best gift that I could give to the universe, my life began changing. I stopped allowing people to treat me the way they wanted to, I detached in love from anything that chose not to see my inner beauty and heart. I no longer neglected myself, I began respecting and loving myself for who I was created to be. I understood my purpose, and began putting smiles on people's faces wherever I went, even today. It doesn't cost a thing to be intentionally kind so I give away smiles, hugs, kisses, homemade candy, words of encouragement, words of wisdom; I help carry things if I see someone in need, I share myself and it is an awesome feeling! I also stopped setting myself up for failure and I began looking before I would leap. I no longer sabotaged myself; I began allowing all good things to come to and connect with me.

I thought about how my children might have been feeling over the years, even though I knew I loved them with all of my heart; they had been hurt too. I apologized to them for the time I did not understand my purpose, and told them how much I truly loved them; I told them they are spectacular individuals who deserve awesome lives no matter what. I became a stronger, wiser, more loving mother and friend. I didn't judge them, I just loved them, and they deserve it, through infinity. I have found my peace and freedom, now it's your turn.

LOVE, this is one of my gifts to the universe and to all living things. But how was I able to move forward in love? I went within and found myself; my true self. I am amazing purpose, and so are you! Let's take the journey together.

LOVING YOURSELF FIRST

Chapter 1
Loving Yourself First

From birth we are taught to love one another; to sacrifice in order to be there with what another person's needs are, but many times, it is at the expense of losing ourselves. We are taught to "love our neighbor as ourselves," and the crazy thing about that is, because we have forgotten how to love ourselves, that is what many of us are doing, treating our neighbors as ourselves. We are treating one another unkindly, and hurting each other because that is what we are doing to ourselves. There is so much envy, anger, and hatred in the world and no one ever stops to think about why.

Why do we hate ourselves and one another? Why do we think or believe we don't measure up? But measure up to what exactly? Why do some people choose in their own minds, to be in competition with others on their journey? What are they trying to prove, and if they are triumphant at these made up competitions, what exactly do they win? Is it really worth it, or is it a waste of valuable time, and energy? Let's take a closer look at these questions and take a journey to the true self. By the time we get to the end of this journey, we will be able to look deeper at ourselves and connect with our oneness of self, thereby allowing us to sincerely and intimately connect with others, and our vast universe.

Why do some individuals hate themselves and others? One reason could be because of their home life while growing up. Children may have been hurt, talked down to, called names, been judged and criticized just for being themselves, and or neglected. They may have even been kept from speaking what was in their hearts, and why is that? It is because man continues to emulate the past. No one on this planet is healed! People just continue to move forward in life not realizing or wanting to accept the fact that past domination and control brings us to the present situations, traumas and dramas of life.

Religious teachers tell us not to worry about what we don't understand; to keep going, without any answers to our questions. Who do they really work for? They teach us that god wants us to be healthy, whole, and complete but am I missing something? Wouldn't becoming healthy, whole, and complete include understanding and being fully aware of the bigger picture as to human nature, the history of cruelty, hatred, anger, where it all truly began, and what it has done to the populations of yesterday, carrying over to the populations of today. Why wouldn't we deserve answers to our questions? I believe being healthy, whole, and complete means fully loving ourselves, others, and this amazing universe. It means knowing and understanding our universe within in order to understand and be connected with the universe around us. After all, we are the universe, and we are already whole, we just haven't been taught to accept it.

We have been taught to conform to another's way of thinking which has confused our definition of love, unity, and oneness. Our heart space is our heart space, and not someone else's to manipulate, dominate, mistreat, and control.

Another crucial reason could be because we don't intimately question who we are. We continue on in life without connecting with our inner beauty, inner love for self, our creativity, our nature, and our light within. We don't fully understand and appreciate who we are; what we have to share with ourselves, and then with those outside of ourselves. We have infinite treasures inside of us but some are not willing to go through all of the debris to get to the precious gems. We are more precious than gold but sadly, many are unable to accept that truth.

Please quiet your mind for a moment. Close your eyes and take a few deep breaths, then answer the questions below:

- Who am I really, my definition of myself?
- Today, what do I see when I look in my internal mirror?

When you answer these questions, please do your best at being completely honest with yourself and answer them from your heart. Then describe your strengths and weaknesses.

___

Now read over your answers. What have you learned about yourself from your answers, positive and/or negative? Be honest.

___

You are so much more than you realize, and you are about to embark on a wonderful journey. You are wonderful and amazing and it's time to see for yourself. Now please go to the next page and list your strengths (treasures), and then list any weaknesses you may feel you have.

STRENGTHS:

    1. _____
    2. _____
    3. _____
    4. _____

WEAKNESSES:

    1. _____
    2. _____
    3. _____
    4. _____

Now let's move on…

REMEMBER WHEN

How many of us can remember as children playing kickball in the yard, climbing trees, catching lightning bugs, chasing butterflies, playing hopscotch or basketball on the playground at school, and dancing in the rain or snow catching raindrops or snowflakes on our tongues? How many of us remember the feelings we had when we were enjoying being a child?

What were you like when you were a child (free, reserved, loving, afraid, bold, silly…)?
___
___
___
___
___

What did you dream about?
___
___
___
___
___

What were some of your fears?
___
___

LOVING YOURSELF FIRST

_____
_____
_____

What made you laugh?

_____
_____
_____
_____
_____

What were some of your favorite things to do?

_____
_____
_____
_____
_____

What brought you great joy?

_____
_____
_____
_____
_____

Now look over your list and connect with the emotions you felt while you were pondering over these questions and writing them down. Did this exercise bring you joy, laughter, love, fear, anxiety, or tears? However this exercise made you feel, embrace those emotions because they all must be felt in order to get to your wonderful self on this journey.

What amazing things did your inner child reveal to you?

_____
_____
_____
_____
_____
_____
_____
_____
_____
_____

We should all go back every now and then, especially when we are feeling disconnected from reality, or when we don't know why we aren't feeling like ourselves because a trip down memory lane can sometimes be just what we need to reconnect with our core being. Our sincere inner child, she/he knows exactly how to intimately embrace us like no one else can. We are still that child; the only thing that is different is our outer appearance and our responsibilities. In all of the hustle and bustle of life, please don't forget to remember you. You are whole, however, there may be some pieces from within that need to come back together in order for you to see it, but for the most part, you are whole and wonderful. Spectacular you!

MEASURING UP

The next question is why do some believe they don't measure up, causing themselves and others an enormous amount of grief? Sometimes individuals believe they don't measure up because they are looking at the world around them with their external vision. They get caught up in society's views, their friends and families opinions, the visions of employers and co-workers, and religious beliefs, which technically are all beliefs outside of ourselves; external beliefs because someone else molded and shaped our beliefs with their belief system or systems. We have never felt the need to go within and ask ourselves these next questions because most of us trusted the individual or individuals who shaped our beliefs.

Ask yourself, what are some of my beliefs about measuring up? Do I compare myself to others, and if so, why or why not?

_____
_____
_____
_____
_____
_____

Why don't I believe in myself more?

In what ways can I begin trusting myself more?

Who would I be without other people's voices and visions in my life?

Is there anything missing that I would like to add to my life?

_____
_____
_____
_____
_____
_____
_____

The next question from the first part of the book is; what are we attempting to measure up to? The only important thing in this world is love and when we get back to really knowing and loving ourselves, we will realize there is no need to measure up to anything outside of ourselves. We will see how complete we actually are, and we will begin to honor our true selves with a peace that sustains and balances us. We will then have no need of tampering with our internal equilibrium. We will see there is nothing to measure up to, and we will live in the freedom of being just who we are, 100% natural, with no additives or preservatives.

Repeat after me:
- I am all I need, everything else is bonus!
- I am amazing purpose!
- I am balance!

- I am whole!
- I am 100% natural, free to be me!
- I honor myself at all times!
- I know how to just be!

Now, it is your responsibility to believe and know these things to be true and correct for yourself. I know they are!

The next question is; why do some people choose in their own minds, to be in competition with others on their journey? It may be that some people may have low self-esteem because of things that have happened in the past or are happening in the present, we never know what someone else has gone through or are going through in their life. Someone else may have no identity at all, so they can only identify with those in their circles; some live in their own worlds, ones that many of us cannot relate to, while others may be on ego trips and enjoy getting a temporary high when they decide to compete with others. Technically, we are all winners! We all came here to be who we are, and we should appreciate the fact that our originality is priceless so there is no need to compete with or copy someone else. We should love, appreciate, and value who we are, and allow others to do the same for themselves because that is the loving thing to do. On the next pages we will talk more about love.

A Definition Of Love

Love is pure affection for other's and one's self; it has no agenda other than itself. It can be gentle when showing affection and it can also be harsh depending on the circumstances and the passion involved. Love is honest; it has no need to deceive, it only has a need to be. Love doesn't manipulate or play games with others, love only loves others. Love is compassionate, caring, and willing to go the extra mile; it helps and shares, reaching out to anyone or anything it is drawn to.

Love doesn't bully; it doesn't laugh at others in a condescending way nor does it intentionally hurt others. Love is playful and silly; it loves to see others laugh and smile. Love is encouraging, uplifting, and supportive; it is there through the good times as well as the bad times. Love is balance, stability, and respect; it is not critical, judgmental, or threatening. Love sees the inner because love views all things from the heart. Love is spending time alone, getting to know and love every intricate part of our being, and appreciating ourselves for who we are. Love grows and has no bounds; it continuously expands because it is infinite.

Love Is Like

Love is like the light touch of the morning sun, softly shining and caressing the skin in the summer breeze. It is the smell of countless flowers dancing in a field, blowing about by the wind. Love feels like a grandmother's hugs and kisses freely given just because you are you. It feels like remembering a time when family togetherness was the only togetherness that mattered. Love feels like holding your newborn for the very first time; you've anxiously waited for that moment, and now you get to adore, nurture, and love this tiny, incredible being with all of your heart.

Love is like long walks on the beach talking and laughing with a friend, getting your feet wet, drawing in the sand, and collecting shells. Love feels like your very first kiss as a teen with the girl/boy you know you fell in love with when you saw her/him for the very first time in kindergarten. Love is like a yard with cherry trees full of energetic adolescents, filling their tee shirts with all of their ripe findings. It feels like a mothers touch when you are afraid of the dark, or sitting on your fathers lap watching cartoons and laughing because he is laughing.

Love is like tasting watermelon for the very first time, and being amazed at why you hadn't been eating it long before now. It feels like dancing with butterflies, in the afternoon under the bright blue sky, then chasing lightning bugs under the evening stars. Love feels like being tickled by your girlfriends at a slumber party, and calling boys from school on the telephone just to hang up on them and giggle because you thought they were cute.

Love is like planning your wedding day, and you know Uncle Harry and Aunt Cindy are both going to embarrass the heck out of the family, but you invite them anyway. Love feels like Sunday dinner with practically the entire family; eating, talking, laughing, playing, and dancing together as one. Love feels like unity; it feels like all of the most beautiful parts of life and lives, all rolled up into one amazing lifetime. Love means cherishing ourselves first because we know we are here to experience our journey by separately fulfilling our purpose, then living and loving together. There is no other feeling like it!

What is your definition of love?

_____
_____
_____
_____
_____
_____
_____
_____
_____

Have you ever quietly thought about what love looks like to you, I mean really? Spend some time with your definition of love throughout this journey, and see if it reveals anything else to you later on down the road. Let's move on to another reason why we may not truly be loving ourselves.

GIVING OURSELVES AWAY

Now that we've discussed love, and we have meditated on what love means to us personally, it is time to think about some ways in which we may be sacrificing ourselves; giving ourselves away.

Here are a few ways we may not be honoring and loving ourselves 150 percent:

- If we are saying yes to people when we really want to say no. We should honor ourselves by being honest with others about how we truly feel. If there is something we do not want to do, we can simply say no!

- If we are hanging on to dead relationships that are going nowhere, whether it is friends, family, lovers, employers, associates, or anyone else. The best way we can honor and love ourselves in this situation is by letting go of the dead relationships, and keeping those relationships that add joy and life to our journey. We know which ones are attempting to steal our energy and joy. It is the ones who, when they enter the room, our mood instantly changes because we know they do not have our best interests at heart; the ones attempting to suck our blood dry every chance they get. Be honest with yourself and clean up your immediate environment, remove anything or anyone who is taking more than they are willing to give, or who is so broken that they want you to hurt like them.

- If we are forfeiting our own happiness to create joy for others. It is wonderful when we can create joy for someone else but not at the expense of our own joy. It is better when we honor and love ourselves by creating joy for ourselves first, then we will be more than capable of creating heartfelt joy for others, and we will have no regrets, nor will we have any reason to hold others accountable for our happiness.

- If we are accepting people in our lives that are always critical of everything we do; those who seem to point out your every fault or flaw by their standards, but when it comes to their faults or flaws, they for some reason, need a magnifying glass to see them. Those who have made it their duty to disagree with you on every level, even when you know they agree but they get some kind of cheap thrill by giving others a difficult time. Those who want you to feel inferior, but you know it is because of their own internal issues. Honor and love yourself by being up front with these individuals about what the inner you is recognizing about their behavior, and by their response you will know whether they are conscious of their actions or unaware of them, which will help you in deciding exactly how to proceed with that relationship. Whatever you decide, be sure it involves loving yourself first.

- If we are giving away money, or things we've worked hard for just because someone told us that is how we will receive blessings. If you have these things, you are already blessed. Sometimes people can give away things to others, to the point that they have nothing left even to give to themselves. You are deserving of what you have because you have worked for it and because it is your life and your choice. We all understand we can't take anything with us when we leave this earthly realm so honor and love yourself by enjoying what you have attained in your lifetime. Honor and love yourself by not feeling guilty for enjoying your life. It makes us no better than anyone else, it just compliments our journey. And if you want to share something with someone out of pure intentions, then that is even better. There are so many other ways we give ourselves and our valuable energy away.

What are some energy drains for you?

_____
_____
_____
_____
_____
_____
_____
_____
_____

How will you honor and love yourself when these types of situations present themselves?

_____
_____
_____
_____
_____
_____

Congratulations! You are truly on your way to loving yourself first. Today, do something nice for yourself.

Here are some ideas:

- Buy yourself a rose, or a dozen roses
- Take a nap
- Have some fun with those you love
- Spend some quiet time alone
- Polish your nails and toes, or give yourself a facial
- Listen to or purchase a great CD
- Take a walk/jog
- Cook yourself a great meal, or bake something scrumptious
- Spend time doing something you have been neglecting
- Treat yourself to a healthy lunch or dinner
- Allow someone to treat you
- Purchase a beautiful journal or notebook to use for this journey
- Go skating, skiing, surfing, boating...
- Accept all hugs and kisses
- Rent a hotel room and pamper yourself
- Watch a hilarious movie and laugh until your stomach hurts

Now go show yourself some love, you deserve it!

Chapter 2
Gather With Those Who Sincerely Celebrate You

First, we will focus on the mental gathering. Picture a table, a dining room table. This table can have from 3 to 9 chairs. Now who is seated at this table? These people are those you know love you genuinely for you; those who celebrate you and your relationship with them. Not the fakes and phonies, but the real deals. Make a mental picture of this or you can write them down on a piece of paper and stick it in this section for reviewing or adding to when needed at a later date.

Blood suckers, negative, cold and heartless individuals cannot sit at this table. Now who is at the table? If you are the only one there, this should be a real eye opener because this means it is time to honor and love yourself by meeting new people, people who connect with you through your heart space, and because you are starting to honor and love yourself, you will eventually fill up the seating at this table, that is, if it's not already full. Always remember, you deserve to be sincerely and purposefully loved.

Now for those already at your mental table, invite them over for lunch or tea, or a movie. You can meet some place where you can all talk, and share with them what you are doing, and why you are doing it. Let them know how important they are to you and your journey, and allow them to celebrate what you are doing for yourself. It is so much nicer to have support systems in place when we are transforming ourselves from the caterpillar to the butterfly. You never know, they just might want to journey with you, and that would be exciting and more fulfilling. If no one wants to take this journey with you, that's ok too! You are never alone on the journey because others you don't know will be on the same journey, and I am on it too.

Once you've gathered with everyone, and it doesn't matter if you spoke to each person individually, or if it was a group setting, as long as you completed the goal, give yourself a huge pat on the back because you have chosen to hold yourself accountable for what YOU would like for your life. Great job honoring and loving yourself and your life!

A List For Those Who Are Journeying Together in Groups

Meeting Places
Library
Café
Coffee House
Group Members Home
Park
Restaurant
Club
Apartment Clubhouse

Things to Make the Gatherings Fun
Heart Cakes
Heart Cupcakes
Hershey Kisses
Coffee/Tea
Healthy Snacks
Pretty Heart and Lip Cutouts to share at will, with little notes attached

Those in your group can decide on other ways to have fun, and express themselves, at your "Loving Yourself First Gatherings." After all, you are Amazing Love Expanding!

Chapter 3
Becoming One With Yourself

This chapter is dedicated to you and/or you and your group, and it begins with your personal oneness first, but you will all become closer to oneness as a whole while on the journey. It is about going deeper within on a regular basis and allowing your true self to reveal things to you that you may have forgotten, or new things that will help reconnect you with your heart space. Now it's time to carve out some alone time for yourself. It can be during early morning hours, evening hours after all are in bed, the middle of the day while the kids are napping, or whatever suits your schedule. This is quiet time just for you to relax, breathe, and quiet your mind. Find a comfortable spot in your home, or wherever you may be in your group. You can just breathe and listen to your heart space, or you can speak softly to yourself. I sometimes say in my mind; "I am beautiful, I am wonderful, I am kindness, I am compassion, I am love, or I say it softly out loud. You say whatever comes to your mind but make sure it is positive, and it is about you and your wonderful qualities. You can do this for however long you would like because it is your time. You can even keep a notebook close by to write down the things that happen, what you see, how you feel, and what you learn about yourself. You will also have the opportunity to share these things with other group members; it's all up to you. Or you can come together in a group and get quiet together and discuss the same things I previously stated. These times will be like true medicine, and you will realize it at some point on your journey. Please remember to take your medicine!

LOVING YOURSELF FIRST

If you decide to, you can also teach your children quiet time, and how to relax their minds. If they see you enjoying it, they will too! Children should also be able to experience some form of peace daily in this chaotic, busy world. With all of the homework, sports, peer pressures, chores, and other activities that children are bombarded with, it will be a great change of pace. Find ways to make your quiet times together personal, it might be a great way to connect with your children on another level. Now back to your quiet time…

The next pages are Journaling pages for your first 5 quiet times; pages to get you started reconnecting with yourself. Pay close attention to the things that stand out. You will begin seeing yourself; it may even feel like you are seeing yourself for the very first time. Come on in, get comfortable, and reconnect with your wonderful self, happy trails Beautiful One! You can come back to the book after your 5 quiet times. You decide on how much quiet time to take.

Day 1

_____
_____
_____
_____
_____
_____
_____
_____
_____

Day 2

Day 3

Day 4

Day 5

___

So, what has your heart space been saying to you during these past few days?
___

LOVING YOURSELF FIRST

How do you feel about it?

What treasures have you discovered about yourself/yourselves?

What has Love been saying to you?
_____
_____
_____
_____
_____
_____
_____

These exercises were to assist you in your journey to a deeper more loving you. They are themselves short journeys into you and your infinite love. You will begin to notice differences in your moods, attitudes and thoughts, and in how you communicate with other's in your daily life. At first they will be subtle differences, but the more you relax your mind and enjoy your quiet times, the more differences you are going to notice. Eventually you will begin to have more patience, peace, love, positivity, and you will begin seeing with new eyes. Everything will seem different as you honor your quiet times, because your inner universe will be changing, causing you to become closer to oneness with yourself, and then expanding to others. Here is a short poem for you to read, I wonder how many can relate.

I AM LOVE

I am love I have always been
Though something tried to strip it from my universe within
Confusion and unkindness took its toll on my heart
Until I rose up and roared I will never let it part
I am love I have always been

Though something tried to strip it from my universe within
Today I'm filled with light
Today I'm filled with love
And although I am a lion
I'm as gentle as a dove

As you are growing, expanding, and changing, you will be emanating the love that is revealing itself to you, and it will be magnetic. Those in your environments are going to notice a difference but they may not know exactly what the difference is. You on the other hand, will know, and it will feel almost indescribable. Stay on your journey to Infinite Self- Love you never know who will follow.

Now think of some fun things you can do alone; with the children, your spouse, family, or with the group; something that requires you to wear jeans and a tee shirt. Create a short list and go out and do one or more of those things. Make sure to try and have the most fun you've had in a long time.

Here are a few ideas to get you started:
- Go to the mall and relive your youth at the teen stores, the ones that always made you smile when you were young. Buy something you would have purchased when you were a teen as a keepsake for your journey (i.e. a book, poster, jewelry, or a game) you get the idea.
- Take a fun class where you would create something as a gift for yourself.

- Go see a hilarious movie, or pull out an old funny movie and just laugh until you cry.
- Go to a place where you can be a kid again, and have a blast!
- Go to a high school game and have some fun.
- Go to a club and dance like you did when you were young without worrying about who is watching.
- Throw a Love Party for anyone and everyone in your life and play games (twister, monopoly, cards…), talk, laugh, and enjoy. Plan a day, and get to it, have some fun!!!

Now you come up with a few ideas:
_____
_____
_____
_____
_____
_____

Come back to the book once you've had some fun. Don't forget your quiet times, and keep journaling your thoughts and feelings in a notebook. See you soon! ☺

Ok, so what did you do for fun, and where did you go? What exciting things happened? What did you buy? What did you create? How much did you laugh? What did you eat? How do you feel? Did it help you to reconnect with you? You can email me at merna42@yahoo.com, or you can write it here in this book for future memories, smiles, and laughs.

LOVING YOURSELF FIRST

_____
_____
_____
_____
_____
_____
_____
_____
_____
_____♥

Now repeat as often as necessary. I am so excited for you because you are getting back to you, and you are worth it! Continue being kind to yourself. On the next page, you will find some wonderful positive statements to speak to yourself anytime you forget who you are.

Affirmations

- I am Amazing!
- I am Important to the universe!
- I am Beautiful!
- I am Loved!
- I am Spectacular!
- There is no one else like me!
- I am the Best!
- I am Love!
- I am Kindness and Compassion!
- I am Complete!
- I am Whole!
- I am Strength!
- I am Determination!
- I am myself and that is my greatest quality!
- I came here to be me!
- I can do anything!
- I am the most Creative person I know!
- I Love myself and everything around me!
- I am Worth It!

Chapter 4
Heart Space

What do you think about your journey so far?

_____
_____
_____
_____
_____

Are you enjoying your quiet times? Why or why not? If not, what can you do to make it better?

_____
_____
_____
_____
_____
_____

If you are in a group, in your opinion, how is the group going? Are you all connecting on another level? What has the group learned from going within, for those who don't mind sharing?

_____
_____
_____
_____
_____
_____

_____
_____
_____
_____
_____

Are any of the seats at your mental table filling up? If so, who have you met and what drew you to them? If not don't worry about it, you will eventually fill some or all of them up.

_____
_____
_____
_____
_____
_____

In writing this book, it is my hope that you will not only reconnect with your inner self, but that you will also reconnect with your creativity; your hopes, dreams, and desires that may have disappeared in the business of life. My hope is that you will stop taking life for granted, if that is what you are doing, because life is a gift that allows us to be the best we can be, and not just for ourselves, but also for our families, our jobs, schools, and other environments; that your choice to be your best will be so visible, that everyone around you will begin sharing their gift of self, their true self, and bring that inner magnificence out.

It is my hope that we can connect on another level, the love level, an intimate, infinite level where we are all seeing with new eyes. Sure there are those that fight against unity and would prefer to see us divided, but then there is you and your friends, and me and my friends, and others like us who are willing to do better and be better examples; better individuals than we were yesterday, or last week, or last year. What makes it so special is, we have decided on our own, to be a butterfly; a brave, happy, beautiful butterfly, experiencing life at new heights, with more appreciation, looking forward to new tomorrows with eager anticipation. It is also my hope that we realize we matter, we all matter! Everything that lives, moves, and breathes has the capabilities to live, love, grow, and expand for the better, instead of living in fear, negativity, grief, and depression. That's why we need to love ourselves first, and then each other.

Who do you say you are in this busy world?
_____
_____
_____
_____
_____

Where would you say you fit into this gigantic puzzle?
_____
_____
_____

_____
_____

What gifts will you offer to enhance your outer universe?

- What creativities/talents?
  _____
  _____
  _____
  _____

- What insights?
  _____
  _____
  _____
  _____

- What truths?
  _____
  _____
  _____
  _____

- What strengths?
  _____
  _____
  _____
  _____

- What ideas?

  _____
  _____
  _____
  _____
  _____

- What new things have been revealed to you?

  _____
  _____
  _____
  _____
  _____
  _____

Now read over the things you've listed. Who do you say you are now? Oh how incredible you are! Aren't you incredible?

Chapter 5
You Are Love ♥

When we started this journey, it began with us coming back to ourselves, our true selves. We learned to let go of comparing ourselves to others, as well as letting go of the need to compete with others because we now know it is a waste of precious time, and we understand that loving ourselves first is crucial to balancing our inner universe as well as our outer universe. We have pondered some reasons why we may not have been loving ourselves the way we could have been, and while some may disagree with the reasons in this book, that's ok. Maybe you have some of your own reasons which are valid to you. I do thank you however, for giving the entire book a chance, and I sincerely hope you have enjoyed it!

We also discussed how when we give ourselves away it strips us of our valuable time and energy, and it has the ability to stagnate our growth and expansion. Loving ourselves first means respecting and honoring ourselves, and our happiness so that we are able to experience more fulfilling lives. We have come to understand that we all have flaws and there are some who are more than critical of us, but it is our choice as to who and what we allow to be energy drains. We also realized that we do deserve the things we work for, and we personally decide when and where to give of our time, efforts, and material possessions.

In Chapter 2, we visualized a mental gathering with those who have been true and dear to us. We released anyone who didn't have our best interests at heart, which allowed us to make room in our heart space for new people, and also more room for loving ourselves first. We now know that we deserve sincere love from others, and we are willing to grow with those seated at the table, or just continue on the journey alone because we know that we are never really alone while we are transforming from the caterpillar to the butterfly in order to become the love we've always needed.

We journeyed through the ways in which we can become one with ourselves in Chapter 3. We learned how to make time to put ourselves first at some point each day, to just be quiet, reflect, love ourselves, allow our inner self to speak and reveal, and to go deep for the buried treasures. We learned how to pull out the true individuals we are, the one who has been lying dormant for so long. Some may have included their children and or spouses, which I hope brought you closer together for the rest of your journey.

Also in this chapter you were able to journal a few of your quiet times and pay attention to those things that stood out in your heart, while beginning the journey within. You reflected on your feelings, thoughts, discoveries, and what love was saying to you personally. Hopefully, this is where you began noticing a difference in yourself, and how you were communicating in your daily life. It takes a few times to actually get comfortable with believing we deserve quality time for ourselves because we are actually more comfortable giving our valuable time away to everything else. When we take a portion of our lives back, it becomes easier to take a little more, and then a little more, until we've found our balance, our peace, our freedom.

Next, it was time to have some fun! You thought about what you wanted to do, and hopefully decided on something exciting. Whatever you chose, KUDOS to you for loving yourself enough to be yourself, while enjoying your time! I hope you enjoyed yourself more than once, and that you are having fun with daily life all together. YOU DESERVE IT and your great vibes are enhancing your life and the lives of everyone in and around your environment. Remember, time here waits for no man. Now repeat as often as necessary and have a ball! Use your positivity statements, make up some of your own, and share them with friends, associates, and relatives because we all should know how truly spectacular we are.

Chapter 4 began with your heart space; your reflections on your quiet times; what you can do to make them better, and reflecting on your group as a whole for those who journeyed with you. By now you should have been connecting with your heart space, dreams, desires, and creativity; they should have been a bit clearer. Some of you may have already started planning ways to fulfill some of your dreams and goals. Others may be taking their time in order to be sure for themselves. Either way, at least you have begun the journey.

We now understand and believe that no matter what happens WE choose to be better examples of self-love, and better individuals; better today than we were yesterday. We know we are the beautiful butterfly we have chosen to become. We are brave, with beautiful wings we will use to soar; we are happy, mentally healthy, and life is worth living and experiencing. We know the world is more beautiful every time a new butterfly flaps her/his wings. She or he adds more color, vibrancy, and life to the universe. All of you amazing butterflies keep flapping your wings!

Enjoy Your Journey

Throughout this book you have been on an inner path back to your true self. Hopefully, you have stopped to smell the roses; stored beautiful mental visions of the trees and awesome skies; listened to the music of your inner nature, tasted what only your individual self could taste, and shared your exquisiteness with those around you.

What we haven't fully discussed yet is the fact that you were already love, even before you opened this book. You were whole and complete the entire time! Someone else's ideas of who we were, and our ideas of who we thought we should actually be, had clouded our vision of who we truly are. You are already everything you need. You are uniqueness, strength, grace, determination, intelligence, success, wisdom, and the list can go on for days. We are the ones who have to stop for a moment and breathe, to get that inner love oxygen back into our bloodstream, circulating and healing us by bringing us back to our true reality.

We have been dedicated to so many things outside of ourselves until we forgot to show ourselves true dedication. When we learn to love and appreciate ourselves and our truth, we are then able to love and appreciate others. We see with new eyes; we love from a deeper place from within, and we accept the beauties we can see, as well as those that have not visibly manifested yet, but may have already manifested in our heart. Life becomes more than just a temporary walk; it becomes the infinite journey it truly is. We are not finite! The journey is never really over, it is just enhanced, and when we realize this, we actually begin to truly live, and we want the same for everyone else. Once you come face to face with infinite love, YOUR PURPOSE is reflected back at you, and it is ever so wonderful! Mirror mirror on the wall, who's the fairest of them all? We all are!

You are everything, we are everything, and because love is eternal, we are infinite. We spend years trying to conform to labels and fit in on the left side or on the right side; up top, or on the bottom, when love is balanced right in the center of it all; at the center of the crossroads. Please stop and know you are already LOVE! So love your inner man and your outer reflections because love is the only thing that stands above all other things forever. The heart has a way of relaxing the inner self to the point of humility. The ego is distinguished during the journey and infinite love takes its place. As you continue seeing with your heart, you will see the beauty that lies within the self and in all life forms around you. You will stop looking for differences and realize we are all more alike than different, and there is nothing wrong with that. You will look beyond exteriors to get a picture of the whole, whether you are looking at the world or every aspect and individual that makes up the world. It is amazing how we actually have to go into ourselves to come out of ourselves and sometimes our selfish nature, which helps us to become more loving than we have ever been.

Once we go in and come out of ourselves, our heart expands into oneness and our purpose becomes perfectly clear. Creativity is enhanced or comes forward for the very first time, and we begin connecting with all things in a more loving manner for ourselves and the growth and expansion of all other things. Faith which is hope then becomes belief which knows; it knows that all things are possible in and through love. And we love! And we love! And we love! Ourselves as well as others, all the way through infinity! Close your eyes and see.

LOVING YOURSELF FIRST

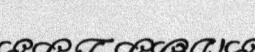

𝓢𝓔𝓛𝓕-𝓛𝓞𝓥𝓔

INFINITE SELF-LOVE IS ONE OF THE GREATEST LOVES
FOR IT EXPANDS TO THE WHOLE WORLD
IT BECOMES INFECTIOUS
AND CREATES BALANCE IN OUR UNIVERSE
HOW CAN ANYONE LOVE OTHERS
WITHOUT FIRST LOVING ONES SELF

WE MUST FIRST BECOME ONE WITH OURSELVES
CONSIDERING THERE ARE TWO OF US LIVING ON THE INSIDE
MOST HAVE A TWIN THAT WAS BIRTHED
THROUGH THE CANAL OF SOCIETAL NORMS

YOU ARE INCREDIBLE
BEAUTIFUL LIGHT
SHINE ON

INFINITE LOVE IS OUR INNER LIGHT
IT DOES NOT BURN OUT
IT TRANSCENDS TO AN EVEN HIGHER LEVEL

WHEN WE GET QUIET WE WILL HEAR
WHEN WISDOM WHISPERS IN OUR EAR

LOVING YOURSELF FIRST

WE CAN HEAL OUR WORLD BY TRULY LOVING OURSELVES FIRST
WHEN WE TRULY LOVE OURSELVES
WE WILL THEN BE ABLE TO SHARE AUTHENTIC LOVE

ALWAYS BE GREAT! YOU ALREADY ARE!!!

The next pages are for you to use for 30 days to continue on your journey to self. Continue being honest with yourself, and allowing your inner self to speak to you. Happy soaring!

LOVING YOURSELF FIRST

30 Day Journal to More Self-Love

1. _____

LOVING YOURSELF FIRST

2.

LOVING YOURSELF FIRST

3

LOVING YOURSELF FIRST

LOVING YOURSELF FIRST

5

LOVING YOURSELF FIRST

6.

LOVING YOURSELF FIRST

LOVING YOURSELF FIRST

8.

LOVING YOURSELF FIRST

9.

LOVING YOURSELF FIRST

10.

LOVING YOURSELF FIRST

11.

LOVING YOURSELF FIRST

12

LOVING YOURSELF FIRST

13

LOVING YOURSELF FIRST

14

LOVING YOURSELF FIRST

15

LOVING YOURSELF FIRST

16

LOVING YOURSELF FIRST

17.

LOVING YOURSELF FIRST

18

LOVING YOURSELF FIRST

19

LOVING YOURSELF FIRST

20

LOVING YOURSELF FIRST

21

LOVING YOURSELF FIRST

22

LOVING YOURSELF FIRST

23.

LOVING YOURSELF FIRST

24

LOVING YOURSELF FIRST

25.

LOVING YOURSELF FIRST

26

LOVING YOURSELF FIRST

27.

LOVING YOURSELF FIRST

28

LOVING YOURSELF FIRST

29.

LOVING YOURSELF FIRST

30

Use your affirmation page daily to get your focus on YOUR beauty and strengths. As for the weaknesses you wrote down on page 5, weaknesses are only things we haven't completely turned into strengths yet. It's up to you to decide when you will move the weaknesses over to the strengths list. You can do it; you can do anything you set your mind to. Believe in yourself!

About the Author

Merna Harrington is the author of the children's book, "Mr. Monkey in the Tree," and "Abuse Is No Accident, It's Definitely On Purpose;" a book written to encourage anyone who may be going through, or have gone through domestic violence. In her spare time, she enjoys quiet time, reading, writing, travel, animals, learning, growing, and expanding in love. She sincerely hopes you enjoyed the journey to "Loving Yourself First." She sends hugs and many kisses.

LOVING YOURSELF FIRST

www.ingramcontent.com/pod-product-compliance
Lightning Source LLC
Chambersburg PA
CBHW070322100426
42743CB00011B/2522